# SUCCESS IS AN
# INSIDE JOB

# SIMON T. BAILEY

# SUCCESS

## IS AN

# INSIDE JOB

### INCLUDES BONUS BOOK
### BRILLIANT SERVICE
### IS THE BOTTOM LINE

SOUND WISDOM
P.O. Box 310
Shippensburg, PA 17257-0310
www.soundwisdom.com
(717) 530-2122
or
www.simontbailey.com

For Worldwide Distribution, Printed in the U.S.A.

# CONTENTS

# BOOK 1

# SUCCESS
## IS AN
# INSIDE JOB

# SUCCESS IS A MYTH...
# SIGNIFICANCE IS REALITY

"Be successful!"

That is the mantra of an intoxicated world that believes achieving success—whatever that means—is the end all, be all.

For years, my entire life and business were all about pursuing success. "Get to the top...be the best...succeed against all odds...get all you can and don't stop until you have it." That was my mantra.

Well, I can honestly say that I've been blessed to experience what many people call success. And yet, I also discovered a tremendous void. There was an emptiness in my soul that I didn't understand. Something was missing, but I couldn't put my finger on it.

I had success but no significance.

I had money but no meaning.

I had power and prestige but no purpose.

I had status but no satisfaction.

I was alive in body but dead in spirit.

Can you relate?

Then I read something about Al Capone, the notorious crime figure and original "Scarface" from the 1930s. When asked by an interviewer why he committed violent acts, Capone replied, "All I ever wanted to do in life was be significant."

When I first read this, I was blown away. I'd pegged him as someone who would have desired success—fame, fortune, money. But no, his desire and his intensity were wrapped up in being significant. Granted, he sought significance in all the wrong ways, but his life is a powerful testament to the innate human yearning to be significant.

I, too, have decided that I want more than mere success. I, too, want to be significant. Rest assured, however, unlike Capone, I choose to pursue only positive significance!

In my opinion, success is a myth and significance is reality. I choose to pursue Significant Success.

The word significant first appeared around 1580 and was described as having meaning, force or energy. Significant Success is authentic. It is achieving life's very best while discovering meaning and purpose at the same time. It's bringing value to humankind—the value that you and only you can bring—while you're here on planet Earth.

Don't misunderstand me…success in and of itself is not a bad thing. That drive for something bigger and better is crucial. But too many people who reach their perceived pinnacle of achievement discover that they were chasing an illusion. After a while the high wears off and the accolades die, and they often discover they're alone at the top. The price of success was more than they'd expected to spend, and their relationships or health or peace of mind were the casualties of their achievements.

In my experience, it's far better to be successful with significance than to be successful without purpose.

Apparently, I'm not alone. There is a movement afoot in which people are discovering that who they are is more important than what they do. Daniel Pink, author of A Whole New Mind, says: "According to one recent U.S. survey, more than three out of five adults believe a greater sense of meaning would improve their workplace. Likewise, 70 percent of respondents to an annual management survey by British think tank Roffey Park said they wanted their working lives to be more meaningful."

Furthermore, a concept known as Social Entrepreneurship has taken hold and is rapidly growing. According to Wikipedia.com, a social entrepreneur is an individual or business that "recognizes a social problem and uses entrepreneurial principles to create social change. Whereas business entrepreneurs typically measure performance in profit and return, social entrepreneurs assess their success in terms of the impact they have on society." Social Entrepreneurship is a brilliant example of Significant Success.

How do you measure success? Who determines if you are successful? Of course, you are silently whispering to yourself that you do. That's real nice and very sweet, but I don't buy it! I invite you to dig deeper, to put your truth on the table and to think about who or what is pulling your success strings. Are you pursuing success for success' sake or to make a significant difference in the lives of others?

| Pursuing Success Is… | Pursuing Significant Success Is… |
| --- | --- |
| Tiring | Reinvigorating |
| Shallow | Substantive |
| About stuff and things | About fulfillment, abundance and peace of mind |
| "Show me the money!" | "Where can I give my money?" |
| Meaningless to some | Meaningful to many |
| Moments of happiness | A lifetime of authentic happiness |

Significant Success starts with belief. Belief is the foundation of action. You see, nothing happens until you believe. When you believe, you begin to think. And as you begin to think about why and how to be significant, you begin to <u>Retrain</u> the Brain.™ When you believe at your core that what you do has an impact on others, you become <u>personally</u> <u>accountable</u> to ensure that your actions are consistent and congruent with your authentic self.

So it probably won't surprise you that this book is about belief. It's about instilling in you the belief that Significant Success is an inside job…that everything you need to succeed and to be significant is inside of you. It's there today, just as it's always been there.

But the seed of your success won't grow on its own. It must be nurtured and cared for, fertilized with new thinking and hard work. The roots of negativity and disappointment and confusion must be cut away, and the seed must be replanted in an environment that challenges you to step up. That's when you will discover you've had what it takes all along.

That is the purpose of this book—to bring the potential for success that's within you, out of you. My desire is to:

- Inspire you…to breathe life into you;
- Uncover the brilliant potential that lies within you;
- Teach you how to increase your self-worth as well as your net worth;
- Prove to you that Significant Success is possible for you at every age and every stage;
- Coach you in creating a life that is both abundant and meaningful.

My friend, if you desire more than success, give yourself permission to live a life full of purpose and significance!

Redefine success on your own terms. Say "Yes!" to your life. Choose to believe at the very core of your being that you are worthy of a significant life. When you do, you will become a force to be reckoned with. I am convinced that when you give yourself permission to be significant, you stop chasing people, situations and opportunities that are incongruent or misaligned with your mission in life and business.

The longer I live and the more I learn about people, success, significance and brilliance, the more I understand it's all an inside job.

***Simon Believes...***
***Success is transient. Significance is timeless.***

# HOW TO USE THIS BOOK

Throughout this book I will share with you my Significant Success Beliefisms. Beliefism™ is a word I coined that means a particular way of believing and thinking. A Significant Success Beliefism is a way of viewing the world and interpreting your experiences that will lead to a life of meaning and abundance.

Each mini-chapter reflects a different Beliefism, an espresso shot of insight, inspiration and instruction, sprinkled with a few cinnamon action steps to empower you to live a life of significance personally and professionally. The chapters are, by design, independent of one another. Each can be read in five minutes or less. These Success Beliefisms are meant to be applied to not only your own life, but also the lives of others. Share them with your spouse or significant other, teach them to your children, reveal them to your friends and co-workers.

Today, I invite you to stop and "Take 5"—take five minutes to inject your mind, heart, spirit and soul with the profound belief that you were created to achieve Significant Success.

# BELIEFISM #1:

# GET A VISION
# THAT OUTLIVES YOU

The imagination is the most powerful production facility in the world. In fact, everything that exists on the face of the earth was first an idea in someone's imagination. When your mother became impregnated with you, she began to imagine what you would look like. When you start to plan a vacation (which some of you desperately need) perhaps you imagine yourself hiking through a cool forest, swooshing down pristine slopes, soaking up the sun's rays, marveling at ancient architecture or studying the treasures in a museum. Every hope, wish, desire and dream is birthed in the imagination. Even you are a product of the imagination.

That's right. You are the sum total of every image that has ever been displayed on the movie screen of your mind. If you consistently envision yourself as an accomplished, vibrant and dynamic individual, no doubt you are. However, if you more often see yourself as inadequate, defeated and helpless, then your potential is wasting away. You cannot rise above the image you have of yourself in your mind. If you want to change where you're going in life, then you have to change what you're seeing in your imagination.

The greatest tragedy in life is not blindness; instead, the greatest tragedy is having sight but no vision. Your inner vision is more powerful than anything else. Wisdom expert Mike Murdock says it best, "The picture that stays in your mind will happen in time."

What are you daydreaming about right now? Your vision represents your expectations for the future. Do you expect joy, abundance and prosperity or disappointment, lack and failure?

Today, I invite you to use your imagination to envision a better tomorrow. The universe is just waiting for you to…

Get a vision of your life that is so big the hair on the back of your neck will stand up.

Get a vision so awesome that your toes curl.

Get a vision so powerful that the moment your feet hit the ground in the morning, everything on the earth awaits your instruction.

Get a vision so big that 100 years from now, future generations birthed from your seed will look at your picture and say, "Thank you!"

…so that it can bring that vision to fruition!

Here are a few simple steps to crystallize your vision and make it a reality:

1. **Write It!** Take the picture that's in your mind and put words, expressions and feelings to it. Then get it on paper!

2. **Read It!** When you wake up each morning, read your vision aloud and meditate on it. Before your head hits the

pillow at night, read it and meditate on it again. Play it over and over and over on the movie screen of your mind. See yourself making it happen and living the life you desire.

3. **Say It!** When you speak your vision, say it with power, feeling and conviction. Your words should be in emotional alignment with the picture in your mind's eye. Why? Because your words carry your energy into the world, attracting what you desire.

4. **Act It!** Start behaving and acting as if your vision has already come true...and begin doing it today. Don't wait for tomorrow or sometime in the future. Remember, when you arrive in the future, you will reap everything you have—or have not—sown in the past.

5. **Receive It!** The vision that resides in your imagination will happen, but only if you are willing to receive it. Keep your mind and eyes open to the opportunities that surround you every moment of every day. Open your hands right now— palms up—as a gesture that you're open to receiving all that life has for you.

I know, I know. You think this is just motivational hype. But it's not. And you know it's not. It is the truth. And if you will let go of your fears and allow yourself to believe in the possibilities, I know it will resonate with you.

I am here to tell you that this is the greatest hour of your life. How do I know? Because I am right there with you. You are on the brink of stepping into your brilliance. Can you envision it in your imagination? Can you feel it in your bones?

I see a better tomorrow for you. Can you see it?

Come out of the shadows of limitation and step into a new reality.

You've hibernated long enough.
It's your time to come forth and shine.

**Simon Believes...**
*It's never too late to become the brilliant person you are meant to be*

# BELIEFISM #2:

# A PERSONAL CONSTITUTION IS YOUR GPS FOR LIFE

One of the greatest accomplishments in the world is to live an exceptional life based on principles, values and integrity. Individuals, who consistently make a difference and leave the world a better place, live according to a Personal Constitution.

What is a Personal Constitution? It is the very foundation of your life, the moral compass that guides all of your actions, choices and decisions. It is your statement of independence to the world and clearly outlines what you believe, who you are at your core, what you want and how you intend to live. In essence, it is your declaration of what you believe to be congruently, genuinely you. From that point, you can speak your truth and operate your life in authenticity. Your Personal Constitution becomes your GPS navigational system that you can use to decipher, decode and define your road to Significant Success.

People who have no Personal Constitution wander aimlessly from job to job, from relationship to relationship, from scenario to scenario, never finding who they could have been during their time on Earth. There are those who will be successful at some level even without a Personal Constitution, but more than likely, that success will be less than significant.

Men and women who live by a Personal Constitution rarely waver on their decisions. And if they have to stand alone, they do. A Personal Constitution keeps you laser focused and causes you to accelerate into the future because you know what you want and you won't compromise your values, ethics or truths to get there.

When I decided to leave Corporate America to pursue my passionate dream of inspiring 10 percent of the 6.5 billion people on the planet to release their brilliance, I started with a heart full of hope, a mind full of ideas and a blank sheet of paper. Why the paper? I had to capture in words my thoughts about why I was chasing this dream, what success would look like and how I intended to get there. On paper, everything told me that success would be easy. In reality, it was hard work and then some. But that Personal Constitution kept my internal candle of significance burning many times when disappointment was almost sure to blow it out.

What are the steps to establishing your Personal Constitution? Well, they're quite simple. Following are five big questions that will become the drivers for your actions and behaviors. Take some time to carefully review them and answer in thoughtful detail. Let each carefully selected quote inspire you.

1.  What is your highest priority in life? What do you aspire to do before you expire? What fuels the engine of your soul?

*Life is a pure flame, and we live by an invisible sun within us.*

Sir Thomas Brown

2. What have you been put on Earth to be…do…have?

*What we must try to be, of course, is ourselves and whole-heartedly. We must find out what we really are and what we really want.*

Nelson Boswell

3. What work, industry or field of study will provide the best vehicle for your authentic self-expression?

*Every calling is great when greatly pursued.*

Oliver Wendell Holmes

4. What are your values, your non-negotiable principles?

*The ultimate measure of a man is not where he stands in moments of comfort, but where he stands at times of challenge and controversy.*

Martin Luther King, Jr.

5. What would you like to have written on the headstone of your grave?

*You cannot dream yourself into a character; you must hammer and forge yourself into one.*

Henry David Thoreau

Your answers to these questions will become guideposts for your life. Get a journal and write down the answers. Revisit them frequently to ensure that your behaviors, action and goals are on target. Refer back to your Personal Constitution whenever you begin to doubt yourself. It will inspire you to keep going on your quest for Significant Success.

 *Simon Believes...*
*Your daily choices will determine if your*
*Personal Constitution is solid or just*
*smoke and mirrors.*

# BELIEFISM #3:

# GROW YOUR GIFT

Inside the soil of your soul is a seed of potential. That seed is your gift, talent or ability. When you leverage your gift, you come alive. You become a spark that can light up an entire room because your gift shines from the inside out. Using your gift leads to authentic happiness, brilliant confidence and incredible fulfillment. If you check out or "kick the bucket" before sharing your gift, you will rob the world of the opportunity to experience a one-of-a-kind difference maker.

Your gift is cultivated in an environment called work, job, career or vocation. When your talent is locked away, frustration sets in—a job is just a job, a business is just a business, a customer transaction is just another customer transaction and a problem is just a problem. You feel as if you must compete against others for jobs, business, sales and relationships.

However, when you discover and fully utilize your gift, everything changes—a job becomes a calling, a business becomes a change agent, a customer transaction is now a customer relationship and a problem is an opportunity to add value. You are not threatened by any situation, circumstance or individual. In the words of Thomas Jakes, author of Maximize the Moment, when you use your gift, "You transition from competing against one another to completing one another."

Living in a constant state of giftedness requires that you fully embrace your talent…that you are so certain of your abilities and your value that nothing can shake you. Embracing your gift is really about accepting your worth as a human being.

As you make room for your gift in your internal universe, so it will make room for you in the external universe. The universe will create the need for you to deploy your talent and release your brilliance. You will attract and connect with those people, situations and circumstances that will enable you to complete your Universal Assignment (your calling or purpose). The doors of opportunity will open wide for you, and you will live a life filled with abundance, not scarcity.

What prevents people from using their gift, talent or unique ability? Weeds. The weeds of self-limitation, the weeds of life, the weeds of setbacks, the weeds of laziness and the weeds of wasted time, just to name a few. Weeds prevent your gift from blossoming and rob you of your future. According to a recent survey by Salary.com, Americans supposedly waste an average of two hours each day at work surfing the Internet, chatting, conducting personal business and running errands. People waste time when they don't recognize their gifts or know how to use them.

So what can you do to find and leverage your great gift? Kill the weeds and fertilize the seed in your soul! Consider the following:

- Identify your core competencies and strengths—the areas where you truly excel. Note that I said "truly excel." Why? Because too many people confuse their gift with a pipe dream. Based on their concerts in the shower, they believe they have a beautiful voice, that they're the next Celine Dion or Tony Bennett. Now that's a pretty outrageous example, but the reality is that many people get caught up in the moment and sell themselves on something that is not, in fact, their gift. So step back, put your truth on the table and be honest with yourself. Let go of the pipe dream and find your true God-given gift.

- Identify your motives. Why are you pursuing your current career or vocation? Is it because you want or need the money or because you're making a difference? If money is the primary goal, perhaps that's why you feel so frustrated. Of course, money is essential. But I believe that when you find and share your gift, you will experience abundance like you've never known. Many people tell me that using their gift brings them a peace and fulfillment that money can't buy. I would submit to you that people chase material goods because their souls are empty, unfulfilled and searching. Share your gift and you will be satisfied—emotionally, spiritually and financially.

- Find others with similar talents and abilities. Study them. Ask them what they've done to release their gift to the fullest extent. What techniques can you gain from them that will aid you in maximizing your gift?

- Embrace and anchor your gift. Create a colorful, vivid, living picture of you sharing your gift with the world. Meditate on it daily. Affirm it as if it is so.

If you're already leveraging your gift and pursuing something you are absolutely passionate about, then I know that you are making a difference, one day at a time. If your gifts are not yet in full bloom, don't be discouraged. Till the soil of your soul, water and fertilize your purpose and give light to your talents, whatever they may be.

*Simon Believes...*
*Nurture your gift and watch it grow!*

# BELIEFISM #4:

# YOUR FUTURE IS CREATED IN THE PRESENT

Not too long ago, I found myself sitting in a session listening to Dr. Mark Chironna (my mentor and the person who's had the greatest impact on my life over the last decade) when he said that each of us must learn how to "buy the future."

His statement bounced around in my head for several days. I attempted to reduce this catchphrase down to just an empty platitude. However, the more I tried to run away from it, the louder it spoke to me. I started to see the brilliant truth of this statement everywhere I looked. The Academy Awards were held not long after I first heard this principle, and I saw its application even in the entertainment industry.

Consider the careers of Best Actor winner Forest Whitaker and Best Actress winner Helen Mirren. These individuals purchased their success long ago when they put in thousands of grueling hours rehearsing, working with acting coaches, soaking up the wisdom of renowned directors, and releasing their brilliance in B movies and in supporting roles to Oscar-caliber actors. Sure, they got some breaks along the way, but they bought their futures by keeping their eyes on the target and being prepared when the right opportunities appeared.

Do you realize that, in fact, your future is created right now, today? Everything that you believe, think, say and do in the present builds and forms the future that you will experience. You buy the future by being the most brilliant YOU that you can be in every given moment.

If the future can be bought, then it can also be sold... often for far less than it's worth. Okay, maybe that sounds like a bunch of hocus-pocus, New Age psycho-babble to you. But think about it for a moment...

In The Bible, Esau—the first born son of Isaac—sold his future when he gave his birthright to Jacob in exchange for a bowl of soup. In today's pop culture, a fresh new talent sells her future when she listens to a self-idolizing "judge" who tells her that she's not talented enough, not pretty enough, not hip enough for America to vote for her.

You sell your future when you believe that where you are and what you have is all that you will ever get. You sell your future when you think that a disadvantage, disappointment or discouragement is your last will and testament. Selling your future is showing up late, wasting company time and resources, and giving the bare minimum. Selling your future is knowing you're trapped in a dead-end job and yet continuing to show up day after day as if something is going to change.

I sold my future by accepting others' opinions of me as reality and trying to be like everyone else instead of being authentically me. I sold my future by believing that the color of my skin was a burden instead of a blessing and that being a college dropout meant I was a complete failure. Looking back, I realize that I started buying back my future when I decided to finish college. I was on the 10-year plan, but I did it. And I'm not done…I'm going back again.

I've made a conscious decision to buy my future. How? By choosing to be happy in the skin I am in. By speaking well of myself and blocking out the negative energy of people who try to project their unfinished business onto the canvas of my brilliance. Yes, I know it sounds haughty, but I was tired of feeling as if my potential was bound in the straightjacket of limitation. No more! That's it. I found my Mojo!

What about you? Are you buying or selling your future?

Ladies and gentlemen, I invite you to start creating your future today. Consider the following questions:

1. Who are you right now in this moment? Are you living as your authentic self or is someone else (your mother/father) or something else (your job/bills) "pulling your strings"?

2. Do you have a strategic life plan that clearly spells out where you intend to be one, three, five and ten years from now? Considering your personal mission and vision, what do you see for yourself when you close your eyes?

3. How often are you at peace? Dr. Chironna says, "Happiness is an inside job." Certainly, external situations and events will cause you to be unhappy at times, but you can always choose to be at peace. If you are too often in a state of chaos, disorder and discontent, you will not have the wherewithal to buy your future.

4. What liabilities do you need to rid yourself of in order to buy the future in the present? Liabilities are limiting beliefs, destructive habits, hurtful memories and other

energy-draining situations that stifle your brilliance. Don't forget your past, but bury your emotional baggage and move on.

5.  Which people in your life are helping you buy the future? The people you associate with either make deposits in you or take withdrawals from you. Limit your time with those who deplete you and spend more time with those who invest in you. Whoever has your ear has your life.

6.  What can you do in your career, business or vocation that will produce results and thereby make a payment on your future? Do you exceed expectations every day in every way or do you just do your job? Roll up your sleeves and identify ways to drive value for your team, your organization and ultimately, yourself.

7.  What are you doing to leave a legacy? Live so that your very words and actions will spark brilliance in generations to come. That's buying the future.

No one can push you to succeed. Many people sell their futures waiting for someone else to push them, nudge them, tell them how wonderful they are and what a good job they're doing. What if you never receive the support you're looking for? Reignite your internal belief in yourself and take personal responsibility for your future.

*Simon Believes...*
*Every action or non-action creates an*
*outcome that either buys or sells your*
*future. Are you buying or selling?*

# BELIEFISM #5:

# QUIET REFLECTION IS LONG OVERDUE

"You deserve a break today!"

The words of this famous advertisement still bounce around in my head more than 30 years after they first hit the airwaves…but not because I'm thinking about a Big Mac!

We live in a world where we are connected 24/7, and it seems someone always wants something from us. People can reach us anytime, anywhere, thanks to incredible advancements in technology. But is this necessarily a good thing? Have you ever wished the phone would stop ringing or your PDA would malfunction? Is it your secret desire that e-mail go down for the day or all the meetings on your calendar simply disappear? If so, then my friends, you need a break!

If you…

… are addicted to your "crackberry," then take a break from it and once again personally connect with other human beings.

… easily become flustered when things don't go the way you think they should, you need a break to adjust your expectations and outlook.

… don't like where you work or for whom you work, take a break to consider your next course of action.

… can't find time to play with the kids or call your friends because you're too busy, you need a break to re-evaluate your priorities.

… have found dating to be a bust, give yourself a break and stop trying to find Mr. or Ms. Right Now.

I know what you're thinking…it's easy for me to say, "Take a break," but it's not so easy to make it happen in a hyper-busy world. Of course it's not easy, but that doesn't mean you shouldn't do it anyway!

I realize that for the vast majority of people, it's next to impossible to take an extended sabbatical. However, I challenge you to find a way to take the break you so desperately need and deserve. Don't tell me you can't find one weekend or one day (what a great way to use a vacation day) in a year's time to get away. I simply don't buy it.

Recently, a friend of mine invited my wife and me to his home in The Hamptons, NY, for rest and relaxation. The first day, I couldn't sit still. I was up and down and all over the place. I'd forgotten what it was like to simply do nothing, to just "be." Eventually, I was able to disengage from the demands of the world and spend some time in quiet reflection. It was re-energizing, revitalizing and renewing in ways I can't even begin to describe.

Just as you have to periodically clean out the clutter in your physical space, you must also clean out your mental clutter. Clearing your mind allows you to be open to receiving clarity on choices, decisions and opportunities that present them-selves. An organized, spacious mind allows the intellect and the spirit to roam freely.

I would like to invite you to unplug, disconnect, listen and learn. Carve out some time for quiet reflection. No laptop. No cell phone. No PDA. (When you're alone, do you find yourself wanting to turn on the TV or radio, or pick up the phone and call someone just to connect with the outside world? Why? Be solitary for a change.) Stop the internal chatter. You can't reflect unless you stop all the noise inside your head. Just relax and breathe. That's it.

Once you've quieted your mind, reflect on the following questions:

- How are you investing your time and your energy?

- Are you making a difference or adding value to the world around you—at work, in your family, in your relationships?

- What makes you tick? What energizes you?

- Are you focused on what's most important to you?

- Are you executing on what's most important to you?

Yes, my friend, you deserve a break today. Go for it...dare to be alone, dare to truly think. Take a drive in the country. Go to the arboretum or botanical gardens. Clear your head and relax. Your spirit needs to be recharged and your soul needs to breathe.

**Simon Believes...**
**Quiet reflection is one of the greatest gifts you can give yourself.**

# BELIEFISM #6:

## BREAK YOUR CRUTCHES BEFORE THEY BREAK YOU!

I'm too old.
It can't be done.
I have no support.
It's never been done before.
Who would purchase my product or service?
I will forgive, but never forget.
Why does this always happen to me?
No one will ever marry me.
I guess this is the way it's supposed to be.
I can't afford the life I want.
I'm going to play it safe and not rock the boat.
I can't make enough money doing what I love.

All of these beliefs are crutches—excuses for you to stay small, stay in your comfort zone and refrain from pursuing your heart's desires. I am writing to someone right now who needs to hear these words. Could it be you?

A few days ago, during a layover in a major metropolitan airport, I observed a woman on crutches with her left foot in a cast. As she attempted to navigate the quickly moving crowds of people, her total focus was on what was directly in front of her. The look on her face was one of distress, anxiousness and helplessness. It occurred to me that one day soon, her foot would be healed, the cast would come off, the crutches would be put away in some back closet, and her life would return to normal.

Then it hit me: Some people never put their crutches away. Instead, they become permanently dependent upon their mental and emotional crutches.

Initially, a crutch—whether physical, mental, emotional or spiritual—is a good thing. It supports us, props us up during times of trauma, tragedy or turmoil. We adopt a certain belief to help us through a major life event, disappointment or setback. We rely on a family member during a difficult time.

But what happens to a leg that must be in a cast for an extended period of time, its work done by crutches? The muscles atrophy. They become small and weak. In fact, if you were to rely on crutches even without a cast, your muscles would simply waste away from lack of use.

Likewise, when you come to rely on your mental or emotional crutches permanently, your spirit, your courage, your passion and your zest for life atrophy. They waste away from lack of use. These kinds of crutches keep you from moving forward with the business of life—your Universal Assignment or that which you were put on Earth to be and do.

I wonder…do people who are held up by mental, emotional or spiritual crutches have looks of distress, anxiousness and helplessness on the faces of their souls?

The crutches of self-doubt, low self-esteem, wavering confidence, purposelessness and sheer frustration have crippled you and rendered your spirit weak. You've hobbled around long enough using those same old tired excuses as to why you can't seem to get on a good foot. It's time to break your crutches and get back to a healthy life!

**Break Your Relationship Crutches**

There are people who depend on others all of their lives and never have the courage to get out and fend for themselves. Take, for instance, my youngest brother. He is in his 30s and yet still lives at home with my parents. He graduated from college, has a job and owns a car. My parents have become a crutch that has enabled him to play it safe.

Why am I airing the family business? Because I want to provoke him to step up and be a man. What does that mean? Get an apartment and fend for himself. Discover what it means to have more month than money left at the end of a paycheck. Stop mooching off his parents. Get out and make something of his life.

I can hear some of you right now as you gasp, "I don't believe he just went there." Well, I did. Tough love must first begin at home.

How about you? Do you have some relationship crutches in your life that need to be broken and cast off? If so, then when are you going to do it? Wake up and realize that you've stayed put long enough. It's time to do something different.

- Are you in a relationship simply because you're afraid of being alone or afraid you won't find someone better? Break the crutch! Get out! You won't find Mr. or Ms. Right while you're involved with someone else.

- Are you in a needy relationship? Break the crutch! Put the phone down—don't dial that number. Give yourself some space. Release the need to be needed and stop being a people pleaser.

## Break Your Career Crutches

Some people stick with a job because the pay is good, the work is enjoyable and they like the people. However, some people stay in a job because of tenure or money or fear of change, despite losing their spark long ago. These people have the ability to convincingly say the things the right people want to hear, even though it's the opposite of what's in their hearts. Their job has become a crutch that keeps them from pursuing their true passions in life.

How about you? Are you disengaged? Are you using your job and your company as a crutch?

- Do you want to reignite the fire within you and release your brilliance in your job? Then break the crutch of disengagement! Identify the real meaning and purpose behind what you do. Shift your mindset. Decide once and for all that you will go beyond your job description, that you will give the organization more than they could ever pay you. Own what you do and do more of it because you love it.

- Are you permanently disengaged, without any hope of satisfaction from your job? Then break the crutch of your job. Look for other areas of your organization where you can leverage your brilliance and build relationships with the people in those areas. Go to HR and ask if there are other departments or teams that could benefit from your skill set. If, after earnest effort, you conclude that you can't find a home anywhere within your organization, then create an exit strategy to release your brilliance elsewhere.

## Break Your Thinking Crutches

I'm reminded of the classic story in which a large pike fish was placed in an aquarium with several dozen minnows. For a time, the pike ate the minnows to his heart's delight. Then the pike was separated from the minnows by a glass partition. He could see his meal through the glass but, try as he might, he couldn't get to it. You've probably heard the story, so you know what happened next. When the glass was removed and the minnows were allowed to swim freely around the pike, he never once tried to eat them. He starved to death in the midst of a feast.

The pike became programmed into thinking that the minnows were out of his reach forever. This programming became an assumption that colored the filter through which he viewed the world. It became his reality. The same thing happens when you rely on a mental crutch. It changes your world view and the way you perceive virtually everything in your life. You mentally and emotionally starve to death despite being surrounded by bountiful feasts, there for the taking.

How do you think? What do you think?

- Have you been programmed to think small and aim small? If so, why? Break the crutch of limited thinking! It's time to think big, be big and go for it. Stretch your thinking; feature on the movie screen of your mind pictures of coming attractions. In order to expand your capacity to receive, you must first give in to something that is larger than you. My life changed the day I finally understood and applied this principle.

- Is fear the program that is running your life? Break the crutch! Don't succumb to the fear of being uncomfortable or the fear of failure. The moment you start to doubt yourself or have a negative thought, ask yourself, "What am I afraid of?" Identify your fears and walk straight through them. When you take action despite your fears, you'll discover they were nothing but smoke.

There comes a point when you have to say enough is enough and break the crutches that have left you crippled without your even knowing it. Don't just put your crutches away in the back of your mental closet, secretly knowing they'll be there if you need them. Break them for good and cast them away so that you can never fall back on them again. Take your two hands, hold your crutches up high in the air and then break them like sticks over your knee.

Learn to walk—and then run—again on your own two feet. Rebuild your mental, emotional and spiritual muscles and get on with your life.

*Simon Believes...*
*Break your crutches and you will never be crippled again.*

# BELIEFISM #7:

# WEALTH CANNOT BUY BRILLIANCE

I recently attended a fund-raising event for a hospital for which I'm a Board member. The event was held at a 20,000-square-foot home located in an ultra-upscale (and I do mean ultra-upscale) community in Windermere, Florida. As I drove up, a valet approached to park my car. The parking area nearby looked like a luxury car lot. There were Bentleys, Maseratis and a host of other exotic cars. And then there was me, pulling up in the "family mobile." I debated—should I self-park and save the few bucks, or go ahead and valet park? Well, the valet said the magical words… "It's free."

As I made my way into the house, I was overwhelmed by the sheer size of it. I wandered through each room, admiring the exquisite furnishings, the exacting attention to detail, the hand-carved wood embellishments and, in the library, one of the most beautiful fireplaces I'd ever seen.

After I cleared the lump from my throat, I finally asked the owner, "How long did it take you to build this home?" Two years was the answer. He went on to tell me that he and his wife had traveled the world and designed each room of the house after a famous place they'd visited. This guy didn't look a day over 55, so I asked him (like most people would in that situation), "What do you do?" His demeanor shifted slightly, and he said without blinking an eye, "I worked in manufacturing and retired, and I've been exploring other options."

As the evening progressed, there was a silent auction and some serious networking. I was absolutely flabbergasted by the incredible wealth all around me. It didn't take long for me to notice that, for most of the evening, I was the only person of color at this gathering. Despite the fact that my name tag indicated I was a Board member, several people asked if I worked at the hospital. I suddenly felt a lot like Sidney Poitier in Guess Who's Coming to Dinner.

The conversations were especially interesting. I spoke to one gentleman and discovered that we had in common some business associates. In good networking fashion, I took out my business card and handed it to him. Of course, I then asked him if he had a business card. Well, I quickly realized this was an "open mouth, insert foot" moment. Apparently, exceptionally wealthy people don't carry business cards. If you have to ask them for a card, it's obvious you don't know who they are. He was polite and thanked me for my card, but his attitude changed, and within a few short minutes, he'd excused himself from our conversation.

Some time later, I saw a casual friend. We were having a great conversation until another of his friends walked up, and they began talking about heli-skiing (helicopter skiing). Okay,

I'll admit it—I didn't know what that was. Once it became obvious that I'd never been heli-skiing at some of the finer winter resorts, the conversation became more exclusionary…and I was the one excluded!

After spending two and a half hours trying to fit in and build rapport with the other guests, it just wasn't happening. I wanted to reach out, authentically connect with people and have an in-depth conversation of substance, but I couldn't because I was on the outside looking in. I felt overwhelmed and out of my league rubbing shoulders with this Grey Poupon crowd. This was rare air and a long way from my roots in Buffalo, New York. I wasn't a part of this money-and-status clique. And if you're not in the clique, you're just not in. Feeling like a misfit, I chose to leave early.

Since then, I've done a whole lot of thinking and a whole lot of talking in my head about that experience. Much of my internal struggle has been about why I felt so out of place, so left out and shut out. It wasn't just because I was the only person of color there. That's not uncommon, and I'm used to that by now. However, financially, I wasn't on the same level with this crowd of business titans, social icons, old-money families and new-money entrepreneurs. I felt truly like a minority…a wealth minority. Perhaps these people didn't intend any disrespect at all. Maybe my own insecurities affected how I felt, and therefore, how I was treated.

Not long after attending this event, I received my copy of The Forbes 400 that lists the 400 wealthiest people in America. As I read the descriptions of these incredibly financially successful men and women, I couldn't help but notice how many times I saw the following captions: Divorced, Twice divorced, Three times divorced and even Four times divorced. No doubt, these people had achieved great wealth, but at what cost? I wondered…had they traded in a life of significance for a life of material success?

On the same list, I found Bill Gates and Warren Buffet. These two individuals are giving billions of dollars away to make the world a better place (as do countless others whose names may never appear in a magazine). In my opinion, that's Significant Success.

After a lot of "processing," I made the following observations in my journal about this experience:

1. When you're up where the air is rare, listen and observe. Make a mental note of what to do and what not to do. It might just keep you from sticking your foot in your mouth. Oh…and don't eat the food. It's just for show. If you do eat, do so sparingly because an event like this is just a big schmooze fest.

2. Treat all people with kindness and respect because it's the right thing to do. How you treat others—especially those who may not run in your social or financial circles—speaks volumes about you as an individual.

3. Welcome those who may come to you for wisdom and advice, no matter their current position in life.

4. Wealthy people are philanthropic and make giving a key strategy in the distribution of their financial resources. That is precisely why the richer often get richer—they give away what they intend to attract.

5. Operate with an "others first" mindset. Find out what you can do for others first, instead of what they can do for you.

Connect with people not for what you can get from them, but for what you can learn from them.

6.  Always be cognizant of how you present yourself. What message are you sending to others? If you project that you feel inferior, others will pick up on that and likely treat you accordingly.

Now, let me ask you…have you ever found yourself in a situation where you felt out of place or like you were in over your head? I know you have. And do you know what? Both you and I will find ourselves in those same situations again. There will undoubtedly be times in life when you sense that people feel they're better than you.

The next time around, I'm going to be my authentic self. I'm going to be true to Simon. And I will continue to reach out to others. If I'm rejected, it's their loss. I invite you to do the same. Be true to yourself. Maintain a genuine, consistent demeanor, attitude and disposition. Don't be influenced by how others may perceive you. Someone else's opinion of you does not determine your reality.

My friends, wealth does not necessarily equal brilliance, nor does it necessarily equal significance. It's been said hundreds, if not thousands, of times before: Many wealthy people are ordinary people who decided to do something extraordinary and stuck with it over time. And I agree with that. But here's the point: It's not about them. It's about me and it's about you.

It's not who you are that holds you back, it's who you think you're not.

You possess God-given brilliance, regardless of your socio-economic status. Until you recognize your own brilliance, you will wander around aimlessly, admiring everyone else—where they live, what they do, what they drive, how beautiful they are. Acknowledge, accept and celebrate the fact that God made you in His image and after His likeness.

*Simon Believes...*
*Brilliance can't be bought. You already*
*possess it.*

# BELIEFISM #8:

# DISBELIEF IS THE KEY TO YOUR DESTINY

Everything that exists, from the airplane to the automobile to the computer monitor, began as a seed of belief in the mind, heart and soul of the creator. In order for each innovation to come to fruition, the creator had to purposefully believe (Be-Leave) in his or her vision and walk away from everything and everyone that contradicted that vision.

Likewise, any business that exists today does so because the founder(s) believed that his or her idea had merit, worth and value. These visionaries didn't have all the answers, nor did they likely have people lined up to invest in their fledgling ventures. In fact, they probably faced many cynics, skeptics and critics who never missed an opportunity to tell them, "It can't be done" or "It won't work" or even "You'll surely fail." Nevertheless, they stayed the course and believed themselves into their destiny.

What about you? Where are you right now on your personal or professional journey? What do you believe?

Today, I just want to inspire you…to breathe life into your situation. If you remember nothing else from this chapter, I hope two ideas will be seared into your brain and your belief system. Here's the first:

What you believe decides the course of your life. As you believe, so you become. You don't decide your future. You decide what you believe; what you believe drives your behavior; and your behavior creates your future.

Have you ever thought about where beliefs come from? Many of them are formulated during childhood when we unquestioningly accept the beliefs and opinions—both helpful and harmful—of influential people in our lives. Other beliefs are created when we hear, see or experience something that leaves an imprint on the brain, and a corresponding belief is downloaded into the subconscious mind.

According to recent research, about 90 percent of life is "lived" in the subconscious realm, while only 10 percent is lived in the conscious realm. This means that our subconscious mind—which is comprised of many powerful beliefs that we often don't even realize exist—is the primary driver of our thoughts, actions and behaviors.

Except for a fortunate few, most of us carry in our subconscious minds negative imprints that cause us to disbelieve what we can do, achieve or become, limiting our potential and our success. And many of these negative beliefs come from the very people with whom we choose to surround ourselves.

I call these naysayers Brilliance Blockers, and their "job" in life is to hold you back. They have an uncanny ability to kick you when you're down, a knack for saying discouraging comments at just the right time and a gift for projecting their unfinished business onto the movie screen of your life. They treat you in accordance with their own self-imposed limitations. In business, if you appear to be wiser, more successful or friendlier with upper management than they are, they will look for ways to silence you and limit your face time with the big boss. Why? They are insecure, immature and, sometimes, incompetent.

Brilliance Blockers are experts at playing head games with you, and they're so convincing that you buy into their belief system about you. They are the root cause of your disbelief. They limit your productivity and handicap your future. They are the reason you locked your brilliance in the vault of your soul and threw away the key.

Should you be angry with them? That's fine...but only for a short while. Feel the frustration, bear the pain, cry the tears and then move on. My friends, holding on to anger and hatred for those who have abused you (whether it be physical, emotional, verbal, sexual, spiritual or workplace abuse) keeps your spirit imprisoned and your brilliance locked in the vault within you.

What motivates disbelievers to dump their poison on others? As humans, we tend to point out and put down in others what we most loathe about ourselves. The faults we find in others are our own faults, whether or not we're consciously aware of them. People stomp on others' dreams and spirits because of their own baggage, their own unfinished business and their need to be right and to be in control.

To push themselves up, Brilliance Blockers must push others down. And we all too often let them! Why? Perhaps because we feel indebted to them...maybe they've been there for us at some critical point in our lives. Or perhaps it's because we don't want to be alone. We're looking for love and acceptance, even if we have to find it in the wrong places and faces.

Disbelievers' thoughts, words and actions, although directed at you, have absolutely nothing to do with you. Their toxicity is not about you—it's about them! The only power the cynics have over you is the power you give them.

Will it surprise you, then, when I suggest that you give the Brilliance Blockers in your life more power—and lots of it? No, not the type of power that keeps you from walking in your brilliance. Instead, (and this is the second idea I want to imprint on your brain) consider this:

Transform Brilliance Blockers into Brilliance Enablers. Take the negative energy of all those who disbelieve, discourage and disparage you, and shift it to positive energy to propel you forward into your destiny. If you don't, their beliefs will become your reality.

Don't be mad that they have turned on you, thrown you under the bus or doubted your ability. Be glad. They've done you a favor. In fact, thank them! Their purpose in your life is to act as a catalyst for change so you can forge a new future.

I'm so grateful for the disbelievers in my life because they served as a mobilizer for me to find my true path. If they hadn't served as or created roadblocks to my destiny, I would have never pursued my life's work. Now I realize they were in my life to be Brilliance Enablers instead of Brilliance Blockers, and I appreciate them for serving their purpose.

On the way from the pit to the palace, like Joseph the Dreamer, we must be thankful for the disbelievers, for all the people who said that we'd never make it, that we'd never last, that we'd fall flat on our faces and come crawling back to them looking for a handout.

Every now and then, think about or look at those who disbelieve and smile...dig deeper, find your courage and keep going! Don't let disbelief stop you in your tracks. You have too much living to do. Allow the Brilliance Blockers in your life to push you through to the next season. What is the next season called? Due Season.

That's right, it's your season to shine. Hold your head up. Allow your nostrils to get a whiff of the Due Season tailor-made just for you. It's your time to come forth and take your place at center stage.

*Simon Believes...*
**Disbelief is a Brilliance Enabler not a Brilliance Blocker—a blessing instead of a curse.**

# BELIEFISM #9:

# SIGNATURE PRESENCE IS YOUR POINT OF DIFFERENTIATION

Have you ever known someone who was afraid of his or her own shadow...book smart, but uneducated in the ways of business; a hard worker, but continually passed over for promotions; always present, but rarely noticed? These people submit to the energy of the people and situations around them and rarely discover their true identity.

On the other hand, do you know people with average looks and average skills from average backgrounds who possess the "it" factor? They walk into a room and instantly light it up. They have a way of connecting with others, thus attracting the resources, situations and opportunities that enable them to accomplish tasks faster and more easily. Simply stated, they make releasing their brilliance look easy.

Why are they special? What makes them different?

Well, my friends, these people know that brilliance is 90 percent understanding how to "be" and 10 percent knowing what to do. They have a certain energy that flows from the inside out...they have a personal aura. The word aura, which is of Latin origin and first appeared in the 1300s, means gentle breeze or breath of air. In the 1800s, the definition expanded to mean emanation or atmosphere.

These people have what I call a Signature Presence. It's what distinguishes them from everyone else, and it's the essential factor in becoming what brand expert Joel Calloway calls "a category of One." They've learned how to tap into and align with their authentic selves. They breathe vibrant life and energy into everyone they meet and everything they put their hands to. They have the power to literally change the atmosphere around them.

Think of Julia Roberts, Will Smith, Reese Witherspoon, Oprah Winfrey, Tiger Woods, Donald Trump, Barbara Streisand and Andrew Young. What do they have in common? They all possess Signature Presence. The light of their being-ness attracts others.

You may be saying, "Those are celebrities and well-known thought leaders. Of course they have presence." True, but having a personal aura is not reserved for the famous. All around you are people who possess a Signature Presence. Think about it: Weren't there kids in high school or college who always stood out, who had that special something? And aren't these the same individuals that everyone asks about at reunions? These people had a way about them even as kids that caused others to want to be around them.

How about you? Do you think there is an aura about you? Do you transform the environment with your Signature Presence? (Always remember that there is a distinct difference between having a presence and having an ego.) Do you breathe life into those you meet and add value to everything you touch with your style and your uniqueness?

The same special something that others possess also exists within you. Are you surprised? Don't be. I know you have that special something, even if you don't see it in yourself.

In his exceptional book Nobodies to Somebodies, Peter Han says, "People need to run toward themselves, not away." Are you running toward yourself in all that you think, do, say and believe? If I could spend just one day with you, I'd be able to tell simply by observing your behaviors and actions whether you are your biggest fan or your harshest critic.

I've said several times that everything you need to succeed is inside of you. This is one of the core principles I teach. And so it is with your Signature Presence. If you can't get to the place where you know beyond all knowing that you are special, that there is something unique about you, that you light up the world like no one else can, then you will forever wallow in self-defeatism.

However, when you connect with your authentic self, your spirit begins to vibrate at a higher frequency. People can sense there is something different about you. Why is that? Signature Presence is magnetic confidence that is released into the space around you. The body is an electromagnetic force field that attracts like-minded objects. (Did you know there is enough atomic energy within your body to destroy—and rebuild—any of the world's greatest cities?) The energy that vibrates from your innermost being is like radio waves that fill the atmosphere. Others can feel it and are drawn to it.

I challenge you today to become a breath of fresh air to the world around you by immersing yourself in the following:

- Discover your mystique, your Signature Presence. Search for and uncover the distinctive treasures of your character, your personality, your spirit. What makes you uniquely you? Your Signature Presence invites others to see you in a new light instead of in someone else's shadow.

- Be true to your authentic self. Are you the same person no matter whom you are with? Or do you shift your personality to match the current crowd? Learn to live comfortably and effortlessly in your skin. Leave an imprint, rather than just an impression, on everyone you come in contact with.

- Increase your energy. Every morning as you prepare for your day, say aloud seven times, "Every day in every way, I am getting better and better." Then watch what happens inside you and around you. Your Signature Presence will begin to rub off on others and spark a fire in those whose light has been dimmed.

- Explore ways to change the atmosphere around you. Start with some simple steps: Be positive and self-confident. Smile! Enliven every place you go with a warm hello, a sincere thank you and an authentic goodbye. Practice random acts of kindness in your own special way…give someone a compliment, bring a co-worker coffee, anonymously pay the toll or buy lunch for the person behind you in line.

- Raise the thermostat of your thinking. In everything that you do, ask yourself, "Am I breathing life and positive energy into this job, this relationship, this marriage, this assignment, this project, this person that is in front of me?" Search for all the options, explore all the possibilities. Focus on what you can do instead of what you can't do. If you never expand your thoughts, you will never amplify and multiply your expectations.

You have the "it" factor. It's time to walk into the room and own it. It's time to take the stage and own it. It's time to get that promotion and do it. It's time to stand up and be it. Why? Because Simon says so!

***Simon Believes...***
***Discover your Signature Presence and let your brilliant aura shine.***

# BELIEFISM #10:

## SELF-WORTH IS PRICELESS

I once heard a story about the famous painter Pablo Picasso. He was dining at a five-star restaurant in a metropolitan city when a female admirer walked over to his table to tell him how much she loved his work. Sensing that he was receptive to her accolades, she asked if he would do a sketch for her.

Picasso grabbed some paper and, with pen and pencil, promptly sketched the waiters carrying luscious ice cream parfaits. As the woman reached for the sketch, Picasso said, "Madame, that will be $10,000."

Shocked, the woman replied, "But that only took you five minutes."

"No, Madame," replied Picasso, "it took me 50 years."

The moral of the story? Know your worth!

Picasso knew how much time he had invested in the mastery of his art. Up until that moment in the restaurant, 50 years of his life had been invested in developing his artistic brilliance. He didn't belittle his self-worth nor did he allow anyone else to diminish his worth.

Just a few days ago, one of my Brilliandeers (an individual who shapes and polishes another) asked me, "Why do people choose to play small? Why do they operate in fear?" I thought for a moment and said, "Because they never truly believe that they are worthy enough to attract dream situations, incredible opportunities and favorable circumstances. They refuse to give themselves permission to pursue Significant Success."

How much do you believe you are worth?

How you value yourself is revealed day in and day out by how you treat yourself and how you talk to yourself. And other people will treat you the same way you treat yourself. If they sense that you are unsure of your value, they will handle you any way they see fit. Do you believe that five minutes of your brilliance is worth $10,000? If not, why not? Haven't you spent years and years investing in your abilities, just as Picasso did? Others will value what you've become only when you value who you are.

For many years, I toiled in the basement of invalidation and suffered feelings of insignificance. I always sat in the back of the room. I tried not to rock the boat. I took what was given to me because I thought that's all I was worth. Have you ever felt this way?

I remember asking a friend back then how much he thought he was worth. He told me in glowing, quantifiable terms just how fully he believed in himself. I'm sure my eyes were as big as saucers. I asked him, "What makes you think you're worth so much?"

"Simon, your worth is determined right here, between your ears," he said, pointing to his head. "You are worth exactly what you believe you are worth."

One of the themes I've heard over and over again—and even talked about myself—in my work with organizations around the world is the importance of recognizing employees. And yet, I believe that organizations and their leaders can recognize employees until they're blue in the face, but the most inspiring recognition comes from within. What the world really needs is individuals who believe in their brilliance to the very core and who can pat themselves on the back. External recognition should be a happy bonus, not the foundation of one's self-worth.

I believe many people are addicted to external recognition. I know I was. As a speaker, facilitator and one who aspires to inspire 10 percent of the 6.5 billion people on the planet before I expire, I had a need to connect with people and a need to be needed. If no one reached out to me, I'd begin to wonder if something was wrong. Fortunately, I came to a place where I released the need to be needed. Now I look within for my recognition. I now realize that I don't have to talk to someone every day (or hear myself talk, for that matter) to feel I have value. If I'm not acknowledged by others on a daily basis, I'm not going to lose sleep over it because I know what I do is of worth.

What are you doing to increase your self-worth? Start by deciding that you will no longer accept the value that others arbitrarily place on your worth. If you're always looking for external reinforcement to validate your sense of worth, you're doing yourself a disservice. Second, commit to spending just 15 minutes every day working on you. Read a personal development book. Study a new subject. Analyze your strengths, talents and abilities...learn everything you can about what makes you so brilliant.

My friend, wrap your brain around this profound truth: Your outward experiences reflect your inner worth. Your self-worth is as priceless as a rare diamond. Why settle for crumbs of bread when you own the bakery? You are worth it! How do I know? Because I know:

- You have skills, talents and abilities that only you can offer the world.

- You are bigger in spirit that you realize.

- You are brilliant!

*Simon Believes...*
*Increase your self-worth as well as your*
*net worth.*

### Simon Believes...

*Success is transient. Significance is timeless.*

*It's never too late to become the brilliant person you are meant to be.*

*Your daily choices will determine if your Personal Constitution is solid or just smoke and mirrors.*

*Nurture your gift and watch it grow!*

*Every action or non-action creates an outcome that either buys or sells your future. Are you buying or selling?*

*Quiet reflection is one of the greatest gifts you can give yourself.*

*Break your crutches and you will never be crippled again!*

*Brilliance can't be bought. You already possess it.*

*Disbelief is a Brilliance Enabler not a Brilliance Blocker—a blessing instead of a curse.*

*Discover your Signature Presence and let your brilliant aura shine.*

*Increase your self-worth as well as your net worth.*

# BOOK 2

# BRILLIANT SERVICE

## IS THE

# BOTTOM LINE

# DO YOU BELIEVE IN BRILLIANT SERVICE?

"Customer service isn't what it used to be."
I hear that all the time…from clients, friends, even strangers standing near me in line. In fact, I'd go so far as to say that poor service is pandemic in business today. As you'll discover in this book, I've been on the receiving end of some of the worst—and to be fair, some of the best—service imaginable.

Let's put the truth on the table: Everybody is a commodity these days—most organizations offer a quality service or product. So how can you be heard above all the noise in a crowded marketplace in a Nano-speed, technology-driven world?

Quite simply, by consistently delivering a truly exceptional service experience.

What elevates certain organizations above the fray is their Brilliant Service, service that moves both the intellect and the emotions of their customers. These organizations understand what I believe and teach: **Brilliant Service *is* the bottom line.**

Brilliant Service is about making magical moments for customers. It's about creating a genuinely memorable, one-of-a-kind, almost transformational, experience.

Merriam-Webster's dictionary lists two definitions for *bottom line*:

the line at the bottom of a financial report that shows the net profit or loss;

the essential or salient point; the primary or most important consideration.

Which do I refer to when I say Brilliant Service is the bottom line? Both!

The level of service your organization gives its customers and clients has a proven, direct, proportional impact on your financial results. Southwest Airlines, the largest U.S. domestic carrier based on scheduled departures, has posted *33 consecutive years* (that's *years*) *of profitability*—even when other airlines were struggling through the aftermath of 9/11 and outrageous fuel prices. You don't achieve those kinds of bottom-line results simply by operating efficiently and hedging fuel prices. You do it by giving customers a positively unforgettable experience.

Furthermore, in a commodity marketplace, Brilliant Service is your primary point of differentiation. Actually, in most cases, it's your **only** point of differentiation. It's the essential factor in creating customer loyalty. Brilliant Service creates a cult-like following in which customers buy from you because they want to, not because they have to. Service Brilliance is all around us. Just look at Nordstrom, The Container Store, Starbucks, Ritz Carlton and Disney.

Brilliant Service starts with *belief*. Belief is the foundation of action. You see, nothing happens until you **believe**. If you *believe* at your core that what you do has an impact on others, you become personally accountable to ensure customers receive an exceptional experience. When you believe, you begin to *think*. And as you begin to think about *why* and *how* you service customers, you begin to Retrain the Brain.™

For too many years, service experts have trained people to *do, do, do* instead of *think, think, think*. Employees who follow service standards by rote rarely create memorable moments for customers. On the other hand, people who passionately believe in their product or service and who are encouraged to think about the service experience can be creative, innovative and proactive. Brilliant Service comes from the heart *and* the head.

So it probably won't surprise you that this book is about belief. It's about instilling in *you*—as an individual and as an organization—the belief that Brilliant Service is, in fact, the bottom line.

When you consistently provide Brilliant Service, you automatically differentiate yourself—as an individual within your organization and as a business within the marketplace. Most people and organizations talk a good game when it comes to service, but they can't hide the truth. The type of service experience you create for customers is either painfully clear or beautifully unmistakable.

I love serving people. I hope you do too. The longer I live, the more convinced I become that we are all here on Earth to serve somebody or something. The degree to which we serve and the way in which we serve determine the satisfaction and fulfillment we experience in life. When you serve your organization, vendors, and internal and external customers, you add value and make a difference with your servant attitude.

Every one of us has the ability to make others' lives just a little bit easier or better by addressing their "opportunities" which are disguised as problems, issues or challenges. You may never know how much you've impacted the life of a person whom you may never see again.

*Simon Believes...*
*When you change your beliefs about*
*service, you will change your bottom line.*

# HOW TO USE THIS BOOK TO RELEASE YOUR SERVICE BRILLIANCE

T hroughout this book I will share with you my Service
Beliefisms.
Beliefism™ is a word I coined that means "a particular way of
believing and thinking." A Service Beliefism is a way of thinking about creating Brilliant Service instead of merely doing
customer service.

Each mini-chapter reflects a different Beliefism, a shot of
service insight, inspiration and instruction, sprinkled with a
few cinnamon action steps to empower you to release your
service brilliance. The chapters, many of which grew out of
articles that appeared in my ezine, are independent of one
another. By design, each can be read in about five minutes or
less. Use these Beliefisms in training, discuss them in employee
meetings, share them with your co-workers.

Today, I invite you to stop and "Take 5"—take five minutes to inject into your mind, heart, spirit and culture a Service
Beliefism about creating Brilliant Service Experiences for your
customers.

# BELIEFISM #1:

# HIGH TOUCH ALWAYS BEATS HIGH TECH

On a recent business trip out of town, I approached the airline counter to ask an agent for help with my ticket. The agent rolled her eyes and sucked her teeth as she said, "You can check in using the kiosk." Her disposition and demeanor sent the message, "Don't bother me…go use the kiosk."

I just looked at her with a blank stare. I couldn't believe what I was hearing. Yes, I knew the kiosk was an option, but I'm somewhat old-fashioned. Is it wrong to want to connect with another human being instead of some zero-personality hunk of metal?

I looked around, thinking there must be hundreds of people waiting. You guessed it—there was only one other person standing in line and at least eight available agents.

I then asked the agent about a seat upgrade, and she had the nerve to tell me that I could have done that at the kiosk as well. No kidding! This obviously wasn't my first travel experience, but that fact seemed to be lost on her. She had been programmed like a robot to send as many people as possible to the kiosk.

You probably won't be surprised to discover that this particular airline is on life support. I've been flying this airline for years and have achieved top status as a frequent flier. These days, flying is no badge of honor. I only share this to make a point: If a business is on the brink of going under, the last thing it should do is tick off its loyal customers! I can virtually guarantee you that organizations whose employees have a "don't bother me" attitude are losing money.

Here's the deal: I don't care how far technology advances. If I have a problem, I want to talk to another living, breathing human being, instead of an automated telephone system that forces me to repeat the same information three times before I can get some help.

High-tech innovations should be a convenience or an enhancement, not a substitute for human interaction. Organizations that embrace, teach and demonstrate a High-Touch philosophy will create "customer evangelists" who will spread the gospel of their brilliant experiences.

Based on my personal experiences, here are a few examples of brilliant High-Touch organizations:

| Brilliant Organization | Brilliant, High-Touch Service |
| --- | --- |
| Mandarin Oriental Hotel—Kuala Lumpur, Malaysia | The General Manager sent me a birthday card, the staff is incredible, the food exceptional and the experience priceless. |
| Panera Bread—Wellington, FL | They bring the food to your table instead of you having to pick it up. |
| Midwest Airlines—Milwaukee, WI | Hot meals and leather seats are standard throughout the entire cabin. This is the best-kept secret in Wisconsin. |
| Ruth's Chris Steakhouse—Winter Park, FL | The manager personally meets guests to ensure they're enjoying their experience. |
| Four Seasons—Whistler, BC, Canada | The service leaves a memorable imprint. Staff members go the extra mile to exceed expectations by anticipating your needs so you don't have to lift a finger. |
| LaCosta Resort and Spa—Carlsbad, CA | Throughout your entire stay, service people greet each guest by name. |

These High-Touch organizations don't know that I'm suggesting you experience their products and services. I was so pleased by my experiences that I wanted to share them with you—thousands of my friends around the world.

As I consider the brilliant organizations above, one thing becomes clear to me: The High-Touch service they provide—walking 20 feet to deliver an order, personally greeting patrons, treating people with respect—isn't especially unique or difficult or complex.

What differentiates these organizations from the rest is their *core belief that High-Touch service is a priority*. That foundational belief drives every aspect of the customer experience from beginning to end, from the type of service people they hire to interact with customers to following up with customers after the sale is made.

Let me ask you, what is your core belief about customer service? Do you believe it is the very heart and soul of your business? Or do you believe it is a nuisance, something that is a necessary evil of doing business?

Today, I invite you to take three simple and yet far reaching steps on your journey toward providing brilliant service:

1. Re-evaluate your core beliefs about service.

2. Identify areas of the customer experience that are out of sync with your core beliefs and make appropriate adjustments.

3. Determine how your organization and you personally can add more high touch to the customer experience.

High-Touch service is a deposit into your customers' emotional bank account which in turn increases their "investment" in your business. When I worked at The Disney Institute prior to launching my personal development company, I realized that people don't always remember what you say, but they sure remember how you make them feel.

 **Simon Believes...**
**High touch is brilliant!**

# BELIEFISM #2:

# CHEAPNESS IS THE ARCHENEMY OF QUALITY SERVICE

I'm divorcing the airline I've been traveling on for 20 years, and they don't even know it.

The relationship has been on the rocks for awhile. Every time I had a bad experience with this company, I looked the other way. I made excuses for them because they were in bankruptcy, laying off employees, cutting salaries and slashing pension plans. I'd been married to them for so long that I couldn't see the forest for the trees. I believed they'd turn things around and return to the glory days when I felt they appreciated me and valued the hard-earned dollars I spent with them.

But I recently had an experience with this airline that withdrew every last cent—and then some—from our relationship bank account. I'd flown into Atlanta on a puddle jumper (50-seater airplane) and had to change planes to catch a flight to Washington, D.C. After landing in Atlanta, we sat on the tarmac for 15 minutes, waiting for the ground crew to retrieve the stairs so we could exit the plane. Finally, the pilot said over the PA system, "Ladies and gentlemen, we've called for the ground crew to retrieve the stairs, but it seems as if they're all in use." Well, as you can imagine, by the time the stairs arrived and I got to the connecting gate, I—along with several other passengers from my flight—had missed the flight to D.C.

I took a deep breath and proceeded to ask the gate agent what could be done. She said the only option was to get on a flight leaving two hours later. When I brought up the fact that the reason I'd missed the flight was because her airline didn't have enough stairs, she gave me that look that says, "Talk to the hand because the ears aren't listening!"

Okay. So, I admit, I pulled rank by stating that I was a 20-year platinum-level member and suggested that certainly there was something else that could be done. She never answered and proceeded to shoo me away.

I was appalled by the behavior of this agent who neither cared about the problem *her company* had created nor was interested in identifying other potential solutions. For crying out loud, at least throw me a bone—a Starbucks coupon, a meal voucher or something. It's the principle of the thing! I've been married to this airline for 20 years, and all she could tell me was to get the next flight?

Soon, I discovered that U.S. Airways had a flight to Washington leaving in 20 minutes. However, the U.S. Airways ticket agent informed me that I had to either purchase a ticket or get my airline to book me with them. I ran back over to my airline's desk to explain my situation, only to have that agent tell me, "We don't switch passengers to another airline unless a flight has been canceled."

I again pointed out that I was in this situation because her airline didn't have enough stairs to get me off their plane in an expeditious fashion. She looked at me and said, "Sir, we have rules...." Well, by then I was turning red (imagine that!). Finally, after 17 minutes of haggling with this airline, they switched me over to the U.S. Airways flight, and I made it to D.C.

Now, let's analyze this experience for a moment: This airline doesn't have the foresight and/or the money to ensure they have enough stairs to take care of arriving flights. That's cheap. While we sat on the tarmac waiting for the stairs, they turned off the air. That's cheap. Agents not being properly trained or having a giveaway drawer to provide a small token of appreciation to premium travelers who've been inconvenienced...once again, cheap.

This airline used to feed me, but then the price of groceries went up. So, I agreed to pay for my food. And yet, at 30,000 feet when I'm trapped and famished, they give me food you wouldn't feed your mother. Cheap! They laid off long-time employees who understood exceptional customer service and turned around and hired workers who don't "get it" for a fraction of the cost, all in the name of saving money. Cheap, cheap, cheap!

The glory days of this airline are long gone when customers are treated like a herd of cattle because the airline is too cheap to care. The bottom-line kissing up to Wall Street on a quarterly basis has become more important than showing the core customers who've carried the airline for years that they're still important.

Now, I realize I may sound like I'm whining or overreacting. But let me ask you...have you ever found yourself in a customer service nightmare, a situation that could have been completely avoided if the company had invested just a small amount of money to provide quality service? And weren't you thinking to yourself: "People, this isn't that hard to figure out... quality service isn't rocket science"?

Cheapness is the archenemy of quality service. Being cheap erodes all of the quality initiatives an organization has in place. It sacrifices the service experience to save a few bucks on the operational side. Too many organizations are still convinced they can make more money acquiring new customers than retaining the existing ones. However, there are countless studies that show the cost of a lost customer is five times the annual value of the average customer.

Consider my value as a customer to this airline: If I've taken just 20 trips per year for 20 years, that's 400 trips at an average price of $500 per ticket. That means just one premium traveler represents $10,000 in revenue per year and $200,000 in revenue over 20 years. Compare that to the average traveler who might spend $2,000 a year with the airline. While this airline is out spending millions in advertising to find more $2,000-per-year customers, they just lost a loyal $10,000-per-year customer because they didn't have basic equipment. Being cheap simply isn't smart business.

According to Jean-Noel Kapferer, Professor of Marketing Strategy at HEC School of Management in France, "To triumph in a very competitive environment, brands must continuously develop customer loyalty by innovating, **improving quality** and maximizing value." He also said, "Brands give customers **a quality guarantee**, familiarity and an assurance that the product is the best in its category."

Here are five ideas to ensure that a quality experience for your customers is not eroded in an effort to save a buck here and there:

- **Take care of the people who take care of the customer.** How? Spend money where it matters. A study of 3,000 organizations by the University of Pennsylvania showed that a 10 percent investment in capital improvements boosts productivity by 3.9 percent, while the same 10 percent investment in developing people increases productivity by 8.5 percent.

Furthermore, according to the American Society of Training & Development, organizations spending an average of $900 per employee on learning had 57 percent higher net sales per employee, 37 percent higher gross profits per employee and 20 percent higher ratios in market-to-book value.

One of my favorite airlines is Singapore Airlines because they provide brilliant service. They spend $100 million annually on training—it's the largest single component of the company's budget.

- **Empower people to fix problems fast** instead of waiting for word to come down from on high. I do realize that in certain industries with strict regulations this is next to impossible. However, push the envelope as far as you can.

  In addition, teach people NOT to just say they're sorry when a customer experiences a problem. Instead, train them to say something like, "We apologize for your inconvenience, and we're working as quickly as possible to find a solution." The customer will likely eventually forget the problem, but they'll remember the quality service.

- **Ask front-line team members what they need in order to consistently create quality experiences for customers.** Keep quality at the front and center of all customer service discussions to ensure your company's relationship with its customers doesn't erode over time.

- **Discover how other companies—both inside and outside of your industry—provide quality service.** Load up a group of managers and front-line people and go on a field trip. Experience both poor and exceptional service from the customer's perspective.

- **Treat employees as the quality men and women they are.** They, in turn, will treat customers the same way. I started flying the airline in this article years ago because I liked the way its people made me feel. It didn't matter that the tickets weren't always the best deal. But now, their service is a reflection of their stinginess, and I'm tired of being on the receiving end of it.

Ladies and gentlemen, what about your business? Have some of your customers divorced you, and you don't even know it? Do you spend more time and money on your brand than you do listening to your customers? Is there incongruence between what you tell customers and what you do?

I invite you today to take a close look at the quality of your service and put your truth on the table.

*Simon Believes...*
***Quality is priceless. Cheapness is...****(I don't even have to say it!)*

# BELIEFISM #3:

## CHEAPNESS IS THE ARCHENEMY OF QUALITY SERVICE, PART II— IT'S ALL ABOUT THE RECOVERY

Recently, I shared with you that I was divorcing Delta Air Lines after a 20-year relationship with them. Well, as Paul Harvey would say, "And now for the rest of the story!"

I received a voicemail a few days ago from Roger Royston, Performance Leader for the Delta Air Lines Crown Room (a business center and lounge area for loyal travelers) at the Orlando International Airport. Roger indicated that he'd just read my article "Cheapness is the Archenemy of Quality Service" and that he would very much like to meet with me.

As fate would have it, I was already at the Orlando airport, preparing to take my last flight on Delta, when I received his message. I went to the Crown Room to say goodbye to my Delta buddies, "Angie & Company" (as I refer to them), who've taken care of me so well for so many years. The team had just read a few snippets of my article and realized that I was referring to their airline. As you might imagine, it was an odd moment.

Angie immediately took it upon herself to find out exactly why I was divorcing them. She listened intently. She didn't interrupt while I explained what had happened during my recent trip to Washington. And she didn't try to dissuade me from severing the relationship because I didn't feel the love from her beloved airline.

It wasn't long before Roger came over and introduced himself. First, he apologized for the poor service I'd received from his company, despite the fact that my service nightmare had nothing to do with him, his team or any Delta employee in Orlando. I thanked him and asked how he'd obtained a copy of my article. He said that Laura, one of Delta's outstanding employees, receives our ezine and had passed it on to him.

After several minutes of discussion, he looked me square in the eye and said, "We want your business back. What will it take to make that happen?"

It was obvious that Roger was genuinely concerned and wanted to do whatever he could to save the relationship. Needless to say, I was shocked and almost speechless that someone really cared. Think about it—how many times have you divorced a business and then received a call from a manager asking what they could do to win your business back? It just doesn't happen.

It reminded me of a story I read once about a healthcare center in the mountains of South America. Accessible only by foot or by mule because of treacherous roads, it draws patients from hundreds of miles away. A representative of the World Health Organization asked one of the patients, "Why do you travel so far when help is so much closer?" The patient answered, "Because the hands are different here."

As I listened to Roger, I realized that the hands—and the hearts—were different at the Orlando Delta Air Lines location, as I'm sure they are at some of their other locations. I told him that I honestly didn't know what he personally, or even his team in Orlando, could do to rekindle my relationship with his company. You see, I'd never received anything less than exceptional service from his team. They weren't the problem. It was the hands at the Atlanta location (and numerous other locations) that were the problem!

Of course, the challenge for any large organization is to ensure that "the hands are different" at every single location worldwide, so that no matter where customers interact with the organization, they have the same outstanding experience every time. That requires a commitment to service brilliance from the very top level of the organization and a willingness to hold everyone, from the top to the bottom, accountable for creating unparalleled customer experiences.

Just today, I received in the mail a handwritten note with a personal stamp from the Orlando Crown Room team. Here is what the note said:

*Dear Mr. Bailey,*

*This is just a "little bone" we here in the Orlando Crown Room are sending you. Please do accept our sincere apology for the behavior you received in Atlanta. We don't want a divorce!*

*Much Love,*

*The Orlando Crown Room Team*

*Angie, Roger, Karen and Laurie*

The "little bone" they're referring to is courtesy coupons, two $50 travel certificates and a Sky Reward of 500 miles towards future travel. Now this is what I'm talking about…this is old school customer service.

Every organization has service breakdowns from time to time. The key to keeping customers after a snafu—and even building customer loyalty—is the recovery. Let's learn about brilliant recoveries from my friends Roger and Angie:

1. Listen authentically to customers' concerns and make it clear that, at that moment, they are the most important people in the world.

2. Genuinely apologize on behalf of your company.

3. Ask customers what it will take to regain their business. Be sincere and look them straight in the eye.

4. Tell customers honestly whether or not you can meet their request or if you will have to take their concerns to others in the organization. Don't paint the picture that you can fix the entire company if your influence is local instead of global.

5. If you can't fix the problem, either do or give something of value to customers to compensate them for their inconvenience and trouble.

6. Share why you are so passionate about your brand and leave the door open for customers to decide if and when they want to do business with you again.

7. Model the attitude and behaviors you want your team members to exemplify when dealing with customer issues. Be "the hands that are different."

I applaud Roger, Angie and the Orlando Crown Room team for their service brilliance. It just goes to show you that one employee—or one team, for that matter—can make a tangible difference.

I might just decide to date Delta again. Everyone deserves a second chance.

*Simon Believes...*
*You can be the brilliant difference.*

# BELIEFISM #4:

# ANTICIPATORY CUSTOMER SERVICE IS BRILLIANT

Almost everyone I talk with agrees…customer service these days is marginal at best. In this hyper busy, do-more-with-less environment, good customer service is a happy surprise, and brilliant customer service is a magical moment. Even in the hospitality industry, where every organization, leader and team member should be completely dedicated to the generous and cordial treatment of guests, exceptional service is a rarity.

As someone who's spent more than 15 years in the service industry, I find that most organizations focus on the basics of customer service—greeting customers, making eye contact, responding to client requests, etc. But just doing the basics leads to reactive, take-it-or-leave-it service.

Brilliant service comes from recognizing the touch points in the customer experience and anticipating the needs of your customers. Organizations that dedicate themselves to identifying the issues that are most important to their customers—and then resolving those issues before a customer asks—will build solid, long-term relationships.

Proactive, anticipatory service creates an emotional connection with the customer. Emotional experiences build emotional equity, and over time, your organization's name becomes synonymous with "top-notch service" in customers' minds.

Let me share with you an example of remarkable anticipatory service. I travel extensively, and I've stayed in more hotels than I can remember. But I haven't been able to forget a recent experience I had at The Broadmoor Resort in Colorado Springs, Colorado.

I'd been in my room less than five minutes when there was a knock on the door. It was Joey, the bellman, with my luggage. I quickly sensed there was something different about this young man…he had that sparkle in his eye.

Instead of just setting my bags on the floor in the middle of the room, he carefully placed the suitcase on the luggage rack and hung the hanging bag in the closet. He showed me the room service menu and said, "This menu is somewhat limited, but you can order anything from any of our five restaurants and have it delivered to your room for no additional fee." He then asked me if I needed my shirts pressed or my shoes shined.

But wait, it gets better…

Joey invited me over to the bay window and pointed, "That mountain is Pike's Peak, one of the most historic mountains in North America. Would you like to know more about it and the history of the hotel?" When he finished, I asked how he knew so much about The Broadmoor. He replied, "Mr. Bailey, I've been coming to this hotel since I was 10, and it's my duty and pleasure to know what makes these 3,000 acres come alive to you."

I was blown away by this fabulous service experience. Joey did such a good job reselling me on The Broadmoor that I gave him an extra tip for demonstrating so much zip, passion and knowledge. My Broadmoor experience will forever be etched in my mind because of one person who took the time to anticipate my needs as a customer and proactively address them.

Does your organization routinely receive such glowing recommendations from customers?

Organizations and their leaders must constantly develop and train team members to better anticipate customers' needs. Consider the following steps to unleashing brilliant, anticipatory service:

- **Hire for attitude and train for success.** For positions that require contact with customers, you must select people with a natural, customer-oriented attitude. If they don't have that sparkle in their eyes, don't hire them! Training can't improve what isn't there in the first place. For existing front-line employees who've lost—or never had—that special sparkle, coach them up or coach them out.

- **Teach all employees the history of your company.** Then, have each team member write down the one thing about your organization they are most passionate about and how they can share that with customers. This will connect employees emotionally with your brand and create the means for them to interact with customers on a deeper, more emotional level.

- **Invite your staff to walk a mile in your customers' shoes** to better understand the impact they have on the customer experience. Create various role-play scenarios where team members "play" the customer or client. Ask them to identify, as the customer, what would make their experience with your organization more satisfying and memorable. Then, ask them to determine specifically what they can do back on the job to fulfill those needs *before* the customer asks.

- **Create a set of anticipatory service standards.** Use focus groups (comprised of a cross-section of departments, team members *and customers*) to pinpoint common customer/client requirements and how you can meet them. Virtually every department and employee in your organization affects the customer in some way, directly or indirectly. Challenge these groups to find ways to anticipate and meet your customers' wishes, challenges or concerns. Then establish service standards that will ensure a consistent level of proactive service.

- **Share positive customer service stories** (from within your organization) with staff every day. This practice creates a forum for sharing best practices, recognizes team members who provide remarkable service (thereby encouraging them to continue the behavior), and sends the message that delivering remarkable service is not only encouraged, it's expected.

*Simon Believes...*
*Be proactive and you will brilliantly*
*outshine all others in your industry!*

# BELIEFISM #5:

# CUSTOMER OWNERSHIP IS COMMON SENSE

A piece of meat…rare and uncooked. That's how I often feel when running errands with my seven-year-old son. We go simple places—the bookstore, bank, car wash, dry cleaners, post office, grocery store, and of course, the movies (a favorite of mine during my downtimes).

The service people don't smile. They act as if we're a bother. As a customer, I feel used. "Give us your money and be gone," is the message from many service establishments. They don't say these words of course, but the vibrations I pick up speak volumes.

Here I am, spending my hard-earned dollars, and all I want is a smile, a "Hello" and a little TLC. Can you relate?

I'm not one of those needy customers who demands that everyone hop to their feet when I walk into the room. I just want someone to "own" me as a customer for a moment in time. And it's not just about me, either. I wonder what these encounters are teaching my son about how customer service is supposed to be given and received.

Not long ago, my wife called a service business to ask that they fix a problem we were having. She was passed around to three different people, but the problem was never resolved. So, she called back and asked to speak with a manager. She was put on hold and no one ever came back to the phone. When she called a third time and explained her experience and what she needed, the person hung up on her. That's right! There was no power failure or dropped call. The person on the other end simply didn't want to talk to her or help her resolve her issue. Can you imagine? I wish I had to make this stuff up, but it's 100% true.

Now mind you, we've paid this company thousands of dollars over a number of years. But the one time we needed them to fix a problem, we reached people who didn't care—people who were unenthused, unmotivated and uninspired to take ownership of the situation and make something happen.

I could have picked up the phone and called the executives that I knew at this company to complain about their horrible customer service, but I didn't. Why? They've heard it before. They already know they have bad service. They know their employees don't take ownership of problems and instead pass the buck. They know that a bad attitude permeates the nooks and crannies of their organization.

Would you believe that we received a phone call a few days later from a survey company asking about our experience with this service provider? You can probably imagine what I told them! Needless to say, we're exploring other service providers and will be making a change.

I'm convinced that an unhappy work environment creates unhappy employees who don't give a rip about customers.

These employees consider each interaction with a customer as nothing more than a transaction. Their thinking is, "There's no need for me to engage this customer in dialogue because he/she will be out of my hair in a few minutes, and I can go back to thinking about what I'm going to do after work."

I'm equally convinced that organizations with high morale, enthusiasm and mojo instill a sense of customer ownership in the hearts and minds of their employees. These organizations understand that customer service is a direct reflection of leadership and training, so they hire for attitude and train for success. As a result, their employees gladly take care of their customers because they have an ownership mindset instead of a transactional mindset.

According to David Sirota and Louis Mischkind of The Wharton School, who based their findings on 30 years of research involving million employees in 237 companies, organizations with high morale outperform their competitors by roughly 20 percent. In contrast, companies whose employees are discouraged and do only enough work to get by, suffer when it comes to results.

To release service brilliance, organizations have to continually teach employees that long-term success comes from owning the customer relationship. Employees who deal with customers on a transactional basis fix problems for the moment (if even that).

Conversely, employees who embrace customer ownership go beyond fixing problems and create solutions that provide long-term value for the customer. These service professionals become experts in meeting customers' needs. The result? The customer relationship expands, bringing the customer back time and time again. I know this seems like common sense, but *successful organizations make it common practice.* And therein lies the difference.

Here are some additional ways to create a customer ownership mindset with employees:

- **Create and conduct a financial intelligence course for your employees.** Educate them about how money is made in your company. As a part of this training, teach employees what the average customer is worth to the business so they will clearly understand that everything that happens in the customer experience ultimately affects their personal wallets. If employees don't know how to save money by "saving" customers, they will squander it.

- **Set service employees up for success by equipping them with the proper tools to own the customer.** This could mean implementing a customer-relationship software system that provides basic customer information, service history and preferences.

- **Empower your employees to fix customer problems immediately** instead of having to seek out a manager for approval. If employees receive a complaint, they should accept personal responsibility for solving it. If they encounter a challenge, they can ask for help, but they should still own that customer and that solution.

- **Ensure seamless transitions for customers.** If passing a customer call from one service person to another is an absolute necessity, make certain that the service professionals who pass off and accept the call transition the customer smoothly from one employee to another and fully explain the customer's needs and expectations.

- **Ask employees for ways the customer relationship can be improved.** Find out what they're hearing from customers. Pay attention, because what you don't know can cost you dearly in the long run.

*Simon Believes...*
*Customer ownership should be common practice.*

# BELIEFISM #6:

# EMOTIONOLOGISTS CREATE MEMORABLE MOMENTS

Eric, a friend of mine, is the Director of Sales & Marketing at the Walt Disney World Swan & Dolphin in Orlando, Florida. (By the way, if you ever find yourself in Orlando for business or pleasure, don't miss an opportunity to experience this tremendous resort.) Recently, Eric and I had a philosophical discussion about how emotion and "magic" are such powerful attractors for people all over the world.

As we talked, I became convinced that in this post-modern, technologically advanced era of civilization, people want an experience that is authentic, transparent, one-of-a-kind. In other words, they want a memorable experience that satisfies them *emotionally*.

At the end of the day, in any given relationship, it's all about Emotional Equity. It's emotions, not logic, that run the show. This is true whether we're talking about a relationship between a customer and a business, a customer and an employee, an employee and his leader, or an employee and her organization.

This idea of Emotional Equity is the essence of *Emotionology*, a word I created to encapsulate the concept that emotions are at the very heart and soul of Brilliant Service. Simply put, *Emotionology is the art and science of making memorable moments for every customer.*

I visualize Emotionology like this:

**EMPLOYEE EMOTIONAL COMMITMENT** + **CUSTOMER EMOTIONAL CONNECTION** ≈ **EMOTIONALLY CONTAGIOUS CONSUMERS**

But is this formula true? Does it work? Absolutely! It's been proven time and again by brilliant organizations that make it a priority to provide customer-centered, authentic experiences, such as:

- Disney
- Starbucks
- Nordstrom
- Ritz Carlton
- JetBlue Airways
- Bath & Body Works

Okay, but *how* does the formula work?

Let's look at the first component: Employee Emotional Commitment. The Corporate Leadership Council recently surveyed 50,000 employees from 59 different organizations in 27 countries, representing ten industry groups. One of the key findings from this survey is that *emotional commitment is four times as valuable as rational commitment* in driving discretionary effort (going the extra mile) among employees.

You might be wondering, as I did, about the difference between emotional and rational commitment. Rational commitment is the "what" that employees agree to give an organization when they're hired: their time, talent and energy in exchange for financial compensation, professional development opportunities and the chance to fulfill their career ambitions. Emotional commitment is the "why"—the passion and the purpose behind the work. It's what keeps employees in the relationship with an organization.

Rationally committed employees do what they **have to do**; emotionally committed employees do what they **love to do**. The possibility exists inside all employees to give discretionary effort. The question is, will they?

Organizations that give as much (or more) attention to culture and people as they do to operations and finances create emotionally committed employees. These organizations are dedicated to developing environments where people are celebrated rather than tolerated. In return, employees are willing to give their heads, hands and hearts to the organization because they no longer have to wonder if they are valued and secure in their position.

Which type of environment does your organization foster? Over time, as employees become more emotionally committed, their brilliance is ignited and discretionary effort increases. Discretionary effort means team members raise their hands to take on more work, to assist others when they're overloaded and to proactively go above and beyond to drive results with customers.

Emotionally committed employees are **Emotionologists**—people who delight in creating memorable moments for others.

Author Jeffrey Gitomer says, "People don't like to be sold anything, but they do like to buy." Guess what? People like to buy from Emotionologists, men and women who are passionate about their product or service, but who release the need to control the buying decision. They listen with their "third ear" (the ear of the heart) and intuitively tap into what is most important to the customer instead of worrying about what's in it for them. Emotionologists become the face of the brand by making magical and authentic experiences for customers, forging an Emotional Connection between customers and the business.

An Emotional Connection occurs when customers and clients believe that an organization (and its products or services) has their best interests at heart. It's achieved when enough memorable moments are accumulated and stored in the customer's emotional bank account that it reaches a tipping point. In other words, an Emotional Connection is made when *customers* make an emotional commitment, versus a rational commitment, to an organization.

(By the way, do you think employees are "customers" too? You decide. The reality is both employees and customers have the ability to invest their discretionary effort into organizations that engage them, care for them, value their contribution and attend to their needs by exceeding their expectations.)

What do you get when you combine Employee Emotional Commitment with Customer Emotional Connection? **Emotionally Contagious *Consumers*!** Consumers are different than customers in that they buy consistently and buy often. If a client only buys from you once, it's a transaction. But Emotionally Contagious Consumers can't get enough of your product or service. They're hooked—just like the person who needs his or her daily latte from Starbucks. As a result, they will increase their discretionary effort by telling their friends about your organization.

According to customer loyalty expert Frederich F. Reichheld, "The only path to profitable growth may lie in a company's ability to get its loyal customers to become, in effect, its marketing department." Why would a customer become the unofficial marketing department for any organization? Could Emotionology be the answer? Customers are looking for—and are willing to commit to and promote—companies that employ authentic people who understand individuals' needs, wants and emotions.

As you consider the concept of Emotionology, ponder these questions:

- Does your organization spend more time driving rational or emotional commitment? What about you as a leader—which do you focus on?

- On a scale of 1 to 10, with 10 being the highest, how emotionally committed are your *employees*?

- On a scale of 1 to 10, with 10 being the highest, how emotionally committed are your *customers*?

- What can you and your organization do to create an army of Emotionologists?

- Are *you* an Emotionologist? Do you work with passion? Are you emotionally committed to increasing your discretionary effort to your organization? If so, then people will always want to be a part of your team or project.

Let's take one last look at our Emotionology formula:

| EMPLOYEE EMOTIONAL COMMITMENT | CUSTOMER EMOTIONAL CONNECTION | EMOTIONALLY CONTAGIOUS CONSUMERS |
|---|---|---|

Differentiation starts with the people closest to the customer: employees. Your ability to create Emotionally Contagious Consumers will only increase to the degree that you are able to create Emotionally Committed Employees, or Emotionologists. The bottom line is this: If you want magical customer service, you have to create magical experiences for employees.

*Simon Believes...*
*Emotionology is the foundation of*
*Brilliant Service!*

# BELIEFISM #7:

# SERVICE LEADERS MAKE THE DIFFERENCE

Most people would have you believe that leadership is about power, position and the corner office. You know what? They're wrong! It's much bigger than that.

Whether or not you have "followers," *you are a Service Leader!* Service Leadership is taking personal responsibility and deciding that you will be the differentiator in the customer experience. It's taking whatever you've been hired or assigned to do and doing it brilliantly.

Service brilliance requires that each and every individual be a Service Leader. Kevin Roberts, CEO of Saatchi and Saatchi, a global advertising agency, said it best in his book *Lovemarks: The Future Beyond Brands*, "It's not about servicing customers. It's about leading them, guiding them and counseling them."

What are you working on right now? Is it important to your customers, your team, your organization? If so, then release your brilliance and make it happen! Take the lead and find a way to make the most of what is in front of you at any given moment.

One of the key distinctions between a leader and a follower is the ability to focus on high impact activities. Imagine with me for a moment that you are the President and Chief Executive Officer of Brilliant You, Inc. Your time, talent and energy are on loan to the parent company (your current employer). In exchange for a job well done, the parent company gives you a paycheck, benefits and recognition.

Management's expectation is that you will focus on high-impact activities that provide exceptional experiences for customers, instead of low-impact activities that author Jon Gordon calls "energy vampires." What is the difference between high-impact and low-impact activities? Ponder the following:

| High-Impact Activities | Low-Impact Activities |
|---|---|
| Create magical, memorable experiences for customers | Result in an exchange of money for products or services |
| Are relationship based | Are transactional based |
| Engage your brilliance to discover innovative ways to serve customers | Condition you to continue the same rote actions |
| Discover the *whys* behind customer dissatisfaction | Seek validation through routine customer surveys |
| Replenish your energy | Zap you of your energy over time |
| Drive the greatest results | Generate minimal bottom-line impact |

What about you? Are you focusing your time on high-impact activities, or are you just busy being busy? Only you can honestly answer these questions.

Consider the eight to ten hours a day that you work for your organization. Remember, each hour you work for your employer is also an hour you work for Brilliant You, Inc. What is your plan to ensure that the majority of your day is focused on high-impact activities? I realize there are some tasks that are important to the overall flow of business and have to get done, such as entering information into the computer, completing paperwork and attending meetings. But Service Leaders make certain they focus on those activities that they do well and that fulfill them, instead of doing busy work to make the day pass by quickly.

Stop waiting for someone to anoint you, appoint you or validate you as a Service Leader. Be the leader of what is in front of you. Here are seven takeaways you can use *today* to become a better Service Leader:

1. Be present to the moment.

2. Act as if you want to be there, with pep and enthusiasm.

3. Answer the following question: "Am I passionate about what I'm working on right now?" If you're not, then make a conscious decision to change your perception of it.

4. Internalize the difference between doing the right things and doing things right.

5. Decide it's okay to admit that you made a mistake. What can you learn from it, and how can you grow?

6. Serve for what you can give instead of what you can get.

7. Seek to be different in your serving approach. Give customers something positive to talk about.

Paul Yost, Manager of Leadership Research for the Boeing Company, said it best, "The most successful leaders perform at that level not because of one or two great moments, but because of the hundreds of small decisions they make throughout the day."

What decision will you make at this moment? Don't just sit there—lead!

**Simon Believes...**
**Service Leadership *will take you into a* brilliant dimension!**

### Simon Believes...

When you change your beliefs about service, you will change your bottom line.

High touch is brilliant.

Quality is priceless. Cheapness is....

You can be the brilliant difference.

Be proactive and you will brilliantly outshine all others in your industry.

Customer ownership should be common practice.

Emotionology is the foundation of Brilliant Service.

Service Leadership will take you into a brilliant dimension.

# ABOUT THE AUTHOR

Simon T. Bailey is a Leadership Catalyst who aspires to inspire 10% of the world's population to find their passion and release their brilliance.

He equips individuals and organizations with practical tools and solutions. He provides actionable takeaways that go beyond feel-good content and produce sustainable results. His insights are based on his work with 1,000 organizations on six continents.

After working as Sales Director at the world-renowned Disney Institute, Simon founded Brilliance Institute, which designs and delivers its own proprietary curriculum for personal and professional development. The results of this work are increased productivity, personal accountability, customer retention, and good old-fashioned happiness.

MeetingNet.com selected him as one of the Editors Favorite Speakers which put him in the same category with Thomas Friedman. Meeting & Conventions magazine cited him as one of the best keynote speakers ever heard or used. This puts him in the same category with Bill Gates, General Colin Powell, and Tony Robbins.

Simon has impacted the lives of more than one million people with his counsel and coaching from the C-Suite to the front lines for clients including Verizon, Chevron, Nationwide,

Society of Human Resource Management, and The Conference Board with his forward-thinking, practical, interactive sessions and action-oriented programs.

He is also a columnist for American City Business Journal. His weekly article appears in 43 markets and reaches 11 million unique visitors to their websites.

Simon was named one of the Top 25 Hot Speakers shaping his profession by Speaker magazine. He is a Certified Speaking Professional (CSP). CSP is the speaking profession's international measure of speaking experience and skill. Fewer than 10% of speakers globally hold this designation.

Simon is a graduate of Rollins College Executive Management Program, one of the top 25 best private graduate business schools in the USA. He holds a Master's Degree from Faith Christian University and was inducted as an honorary member of the University of Central Florida Golden Key International Honor Society. Simon and his family reside in a small quaint town of 2,500 residents and a few dirt roads in Windermere, Florida, USA, where he works on his tan year round.

**Educational Resources from Simon T. Bailey and Brilliance Institute, Inc.**

Sign up for my free weekly brilliance newsletter—
www.simontbailey.com

Simon's blog: www.simontbailey.com/blog

Building Business Relationships by Simon T. Bailey—
7 Day Free Trial www.lynda.com/trial/SimonTBailey

Follow me:
www.twitter.com/simontbailey

Simon's YouTube channel:
www.youtube.com/simontbailey

Link with Simon T. Bailey:
www.linkedin.com/in/simontbailey

Become a Fan of Simon T. Bailey—
https://www.facebook.com/SimonTBrillionaire

Download the Simon T. Bailey App at
www.simontbailey.com

Request the free e-book, *Meditate on Your Personal
Brilliance*, by e-mailing hello@simontbailey.com

# EBOOKS BY SIMON T. BAILEY

*Simon Says Dream: Live a Passionate Life*—This was the first book I released when I left Disney. Serena and Venus Williams were some of the first celebrities to read it. http://ow.ly/qljPZ

*Success is an Inside Job*—I wrote this book from a deep place and really had to live it. In other words, I had to live it from the inside out. http://ow.ly/qljSG

*Meditate on Your Professional Brilliance*—These are pithy one liners and sound bites that will help you get through the day. http://ow.ly/qljUP

*Brilliant Service is the Bottom Line*—Everything I learned from Disney and from working with over 1,000 organizations—everything I discovered about the awesomeness of customer experience—is included in this book. http://ow.ly/qljXF

*Meditate on Your Personal Brilliance*—This was written out of my struggle with wanting to know how to shift my thinking and live a meaningful life. http://ow.ly/qlk31

### For More Information

To inquire about having Simon T. Bailey
speak at your next meeting:

Please e-mail hello@simontbailey.com

Website—www.simontbailey.com

Connect with Simon T. Bailey

Twitter—@simontbailey

Facebook—Simon T. Bailey

LinkedIn—Simon T. Bailey

## Are you ready to live your full potential?

Simon's *Shift Your Brilliance System* will teach you to see differently:

- See Yourself Differently
- See Your Ideas Differently
- See Your Job/Business Differently
- See Customer Service Differently

Discover a fresh vision of your brilliance.

You will learn to recognize opportunities and perform at a higher level in areas that matter most to you.

This course also works well as a group project as you go through the seven steps to shift your brilliance with your friends or co-workers.

Learn more at: **www.shiftyourbrilliance.com**